No weap
against your marriage
will prosper.

Your Marriage is Worth
Fighting For

Laura T. Gethers

Laura T. Gethers

Copyright

Introduction

This devotional that you are about to read is a result of my being intentional about spending time with God, intentional about hearing His voice, and intentional about completing a task that He placed on my heart. I realized that marriage became a part of my purpose the moment I decided I wanted to say, "I do". I have spent countless hours praying and reading the word of God to gain a deeper understanding about marriage.

My hope in writing this devotional is that you will choose to always fight for your marriage. Do not allow divorce to be the solution to the hardships you will face. The institution of marriage is under attack; Satan seeks to destroy it, and I want married couples to remember that you *wrestle not against flesh and blood, but against principalities, against powers, against the rulers of the darkness of this world, against spiritual wickedness in high places.* Let this devotional remind you to attack the issue and not each other. May you be encouraged to use one of the mightiest weapons you have been given, prayer.

Take the scriptures in this devotional and study them for yourself. Ask God to give you understanding on how to apply the scriptures to your life, and to your marriage. Use the lines provided after each devotional entry to write down your thoughts or plans on how to incorporate the scriptures. I have included a thirty-day challenge at the end of the devotional to give you some ideas on how to connect with your spouse and strengthen your marriage; feel free to use those ideas or come up with some on your own.

Table of Contents

Day 1
Inseparable Love

So they are no longer two but one flesh, what therefore God joined together let no man separate.
-Matthew 19:6

During premarital counseling Shanel was given a salt shaker and Shane a pepper shaker. There was an empty container on the table. Shane and Shanel were told to pour the salt and pepper into the container and shake it up. Next, they were asked to separate the salt from the pepper. The couple tried, but were unsuccessful in their efforts. The counselor told Shane and Shanel to take the salt and pepper mixture home and keep the container in a visible place to remind them that nothing should be able to separate them. Lastly, the counselor told them that they would most likely face issues in their marriage that would make them consider separation or even divorce. She reminded them to fight for their marriage and not look to separation or divorce as the solution to their issues.

After their wedding Shanel and Shane quickly realized the counselor was right about things causing them to consider separation. First, there was Shane's new job. He was expected to arrive early, stay late, and work on the weekends. His demanding work schedule was causing a lot of arguments due to his inability to spend time with his wife. He knew he had two options: find a new job, or let his work separate him from his wife. He chose to find a new job that allowed him to have a good work/life balance. The next challenge came when Shanel's friends wanted her to leave Shane home alone and spend every weekend hanging out with them. They would get upset with her and try to make her feel bad when she chose to stay home. Eventually, she decided to address the situation. She told them that she loved them and enjoyed their time together but her marriage was her first priority. The conversation resulted in them picking one weekend a month to spend time together.

On your wedding day, it is hard to imagine that anything could cause you to separate from your spouse. Unfortunately, obstacles come in many forms to try to divide you. It is up to you and your spouse to protect your marriage. So, before you agree to accept a demanding job make sure your spouse is in agreement with your decision. When your friends call to invite you out for the weekend, consult with your spouse before you accept. When you get married, your spouse becomes your first priority. You should not allow your job, friends, or anything else to put you against your spouse. It is your responsibility to protect your marriage.

Love Note
When you get married your spouse becomes your first priority.

Prayer:

Father,

May I remember that nothing should be able to separate me from my spouse. May I always consider my spouse when making any decision. If a decision is not in the best interest for both of us may I walk away from it. Remind me of the commitment I made on my wedding day. Remind me of the responsibility I have in regard to my spouse. May I truly become one in my thoughts, actions, and words with my spouse. In Jesus' name, I pray.

Amen!

Personal Notes

_____

_____

_____

_____

_____

_____

Day 2
Husbandly Love

Husbands, love your wives, just as Christ also loved the church and gave Himself up for her.... So husbands ought to love their own wives as their own bodies; he who loves his wife loves himself.
-Ephesians 5:25, 28 (NKJV)

Michael was so excited to leave work and go home to tell his wife Maura about his promotion. It meant that they would have to leave Florida and move to North Carolina, but it also meant he finally had the opportunity to pursue his dream job. Michael pulled into the driveway and then raced toward the house when he saw Maura standing at the front door with this huge smile on her face. She said, "Honey, I have the most amazing news." Michael replied, "So do I." They went back and forth about who would go first. Finally, Maura said, "I received my acceptance letter for medical school; I start next semester." Michael knew this was a dream come true for Maura. He knew how badly she wanted to get into that particular school. Maura had worked so hard for this opportunity, and he did not want her to pass it up. He knew that he would have to put his dreams on hold so that his wife could pursue hers. Michael shared his good news with Maura, but immediately told her he would turn down the promotion, so that she could attend medical school. Maura pulled him close and kissed him. She thanked him for being willing to sacrifice his dreams so that she could pursue hers.

Would you be willing to sacrifice a job or promotion so that your spouse could pursue their dreams? Would you be willing to give up some of that precious "me" time to help do yard work? Or give up that bad habit so that your marriage can be restored? Are you willing to lay down your life for your spouse?

Eventually you will be faced with the choice of having to "lay down" something for your spouse. Your marriage is going to cost you something. After all, marriage is supposed to be a reflection of Christ's relationship with the church, and it cost him his life. The sacrifices you make in your marriage will benefit both you and your

7

spouse in the long run. Every time you invest in your spouse, you are investing in yourself.

Love Note
The sacrifices you make in your marriage will benefit both you and your spouse in the long run.

Prayer:

Father,

Help me truly understand what it means to love my spouse like Christ loves the church. May I be willing to sacrifice anything you tell me to for my spouse. Help me lay aside pride, greed or anything that would prevent me from loving my spouse as I love myself. Destroy any preconceived ideas I have on what my role is in this marriage and let me seek out your will. Teach me how to love like Christ loved; teach me how to lead like Christ led. Give me the confidence and wisdom to be who I was created to be in this marriage. In Jesus' name, I pray.

Amen!

Personal Notes

_____

_____

_____

_____

_____

_____

Day 3
Wifely Love

Wives, submit to your husbands as to the Lord. For the husband is the head of the wife as Christ is the head of the church, his body, of which he is the Savior. Now as the church submits to Christ, so also wives should submit to their husbands in everything.
-Ephesians 5:22-24 (NIV)

Susan and Samuel are newlyweds. They have been married for a year now. Susan was excited about marriage, but she became nervous after hearing a lot of horror stories from wives about submission. She heard how most wives fail at it terribly and how it was nothing but a way for men to control their wives. Susan knew that the bible spoke of submission. She knew that she wanted to be the wife God created her to be. Therefore, Susan studied about submission; she even questioned wives as to why they thought it was so hard. Then she developed a three-part plan that would help her be submissive. Her first step was to hear her husband's point of view without interrupting. Next, she would state her thoughts on the topic. Lastly, she would submit as long as it did not cause her to sin against God.

Susan's first encounter with submission came when she and her husband disagreed about the way they should handle their finances. Samuel thought they should have one main account in which all their bills were deducted. Susan thought they should have one account for bills and then a separate savings account. Though her plan was different, she thought her husband's plan could work, so she agreed to try things his way. The second encounter came when they had to decide whether they would buy or rent a house. Samuel wanted to rent while Susan wanted to buy. They both had very good reasons for their choice, but once again Susan yielded. A third encounter came when they had to decide which church to attend. Susan loved attending her family's church. She had been there all her life. She would not entertain the thought of visiting another church or even listen to why Samuel wanted to visit other churches. Weeks later, Susan was reviewing her submission plan and concluded, that she was willing to submit to her husband in some areas and not others.

She wanted to be the wife God created her to be. She realized submission was bigger than her three-part plan; she needed God to guide her every day. Therefore, she started spending time with God so He could show her how to submit.

Did you rejoice the first time you heard about submission? Maybe your response was something like, "Submit to whom? I am not going to let anyone think they can tell me what to do." Maybe you feel like your spouse is not worthy of your submission.

The word submission has been looked upon as something bad. That is so far from the truth. Submission is not easy, but it does not have to be as difficult as it is made out to be. As a wife, when you choose to submit, you give your spouse the power to fulfill their role as your husband. You are yielding to what you and your husband think is best. It does not mean that you cannot present different ideas or solutions. It does not mean that you nod your head in agreement with everything your husband says. It means that you allow your husband to take responsibility for your family, trusting that he will listen and follow God.

Ephesians 5:21 states that spouses are to *submit to one another out of reverence for Christ*. That means as a spouse you cannot pick and choose which areas you are going to submit. You may have to relinquish some power but that does not make you weak. It makes you strong. Being able to submit shows your real strength and your ability to trust someone other than yourself. All of these character traits are important in building a strong marriage.

Love Note
Being able to submit shows your real strength.

Prayer:

Father,

In the name of Jesus, I thank you for your example of submission when you went to the cross and submitted your life for me! Teach me how to submit, give me the true definition of what submission is and how to apply it to my relationship with you and my spouse. Show me the areas that I have not submitted to you and my spouse. I know that your thoughts towards me are precious so you would not tell me to do something that would hurt me, enslave me, or belittle me. So teach me, Lord, how to move past my wrongful thoughts concerning submission. Your ways and thoughts are higher than mine so I trust you to lead me in my marriage. In Jesus' name, I pray.

Amen!

Personal Notes

_____

_____

_____

_____

_____

_____

Day 4
Patient Love
Love is patient.....
-1 Corinthians 13:4 (NIV)

Juliette and her husband John are polar opposites when it comes to their ability to stay focused and make decisions. At a very young age Juliette knew she wanted to become a lawyer. She worked hard in high school, completed both her undergraduate program and law school. Now, she has her own practice and has made quite a name for herself. Whether at work or at home she makes a list of what must be done and then does it. She takes a "no excuse" approach in life. Now, John is a bit more relaxed; he is what some would call "a jack of all trades but master of none," jumping from job to job. In the past five years, he has been a restaurant manager, pastry chef, and now he wants to buy a food truck. Juliette is decisive; if they go shopping, she knows what she is going to buy before she goes into the store. Unless there are long lines to contend with, Juliette is in and out within five minutes. John, on the other hand, visits ten different stores at the mall not knowing what exactly he is looking to purchase. He may wait in a long line and then, when he reaches the register, decides he doesn't want to buy anything.

When they first met, Juliette admired John's free spirit; it was one of the things that attracted her to him. Now that they are making decisions together, such as what house to buy and when to have children, Juliette is starting to grow impatient with John's indecisiveness and lack of focus. She wants John to find a more stable career and help make the important decisions. John does not understand why everything must be planned out; he wants to go with the flow. He suggests that Juliette stop using birth control allow things to happen naturally in their timing; and when they see a house they like, they will make an offer. Juliette has found herself praying for more and more patience. Nevertheless, she often finds herself yelling at John and complaining about his indecisiveness.

Are you like Juliette? Do you plan everything out? Do you know what you want and you go after it, but have a spouse that is much like John, lacking focus? Do you often find yourself growing impatient with your spouse's inability to make a decision and/or lack of consistency? Have you tried being patient or praying for patience, only to find yourself becoming more impatient?

Maybe you have the wrong idea of what being patient means. After all, being patient is more than waiting for someone or something to change. It is a mindset and an attitude. You must be able to remain consistent in your emotions and actions while waiting. So, if you know that your spouse takes a long time to make a decision, do not wait until the last minute when a decision needs to be made; give your spouse time to make a decision. If your spouse is indecisive, do not give them a lot of options when having to make a choice. For example, when planning dinner, only present two options versus five. This will decrease your level of frustration, and help you in your effort to become more patient.

Loving your spouse is going to require patience. This can be very difficult, especially when you are dealing with an indecisive spouse. Nevertheless, you vowed to be patient with your spouse the day you decided to marry. If this is a challenge for you, begin to remind yourself of the areas in which you have struggled, and how patient God has been with you. Eat a big slice of humble pie, and then ask God to help you be as patient with your spouse as He is with you.

Love Note
Loving your spouse is going to require patience.

Prayer:

Father,

Teach me how to be patient with my spouse. May I trust in your perfect timing instead of wanting things to change in my timing. Help me to put my trust in you and not give up or complain every time I do not see the change in my spouse that I have been praying for. Instead show me how I can change my words, my thinking, and my heart concerning the situation. In Jesus' name, I pray.

Amen!

Personal Notes

_____

_____

_____

_____

_____

_____

Day 5
Kind Love
Love is kind
-1 Corinthians 13:4 (NIV)

Most of her life Rebecca has struggled with being affectionate. She grew up being the only girl amongst five boys. She developed a thick skin as her brothers constantly picked on her. Therefore, she is not the "touchy-feely" type of person. She does not like hugs or kisses. Rebecca married Robert, who loves to give her big bear hugs and kisses all the time. When Robert tries to display this type of affection towards her, she becomes very abrasive. She pushes him away and often leaves the room. Robert desires nothing more than to have his wife welcome his hugs and kisses but also wants to respect her feelings. He understands that Rebecca struggles showing affection, and he accepted that before they got married. He remains hopeful that one day she will show him love the way he desires it.

Rebecca loves Robert, but she has a hard time displaying affection. She would rather display her love for him through cooking, cleaning, and taking care of the finances for their home. She knows that Robert desires affection, but she is trying to show him that she loves him the best way that she can. The way that she is comfortable expressing her love.

How do you show love to your spouse? The scripture above states that "love is kind." It does not say love is always comfortable. You may not be comfortable showing affection to your spouse or giving compliments, but if that is the way that your spouse receives love then it is something you should strive to do. It is just as important for you to do something that your spouse would receive as an act of kindness as it is for you to be kind. So, instead of just doing random acts of kindness, take time to study your spouse. Ask them questions and see what they would enjoy. For some, it may be showing affection or sitting and watching a sports game or movie. For others, it may be bringing home flowers or washing the dishes. Make sure you are intentional about finding out what your spouse likes or wants from you and then do it. Do not be afraid or ashamed to seek professional help if you are really struggling with meeting your spouse's needs. If you want to learn more about how your spouse receives love check out Gary Chapman's "The Five Love Languages" quiz at http://www.5lovelanguages.com/profile/.

Love Note

Make sure you are intentional about finding out what your spouse likes or wants from you and then do it.

Prayer:

Father,

Show me how to be kind to my spouse. Teach me to think about the things they enjoy. May my acts of kindness be a true reflection of the love I have for my spouse. May I be willing to sacrifice my time, feelings and comfort to show my appreciation. In Jesus' name, I pray!

Amen!

Personal Notes

_____

_____

_____

_____

_____

_____

Day 6
Jealous Love
(Love) *is not jealous;*
-1 Corinthians 13:4

Dan and Deborah had just come home from a double date with their dear friends Morris and Mandy. When they approached their home, Dan opened the door and walked in ahead of Deborah. Deborah stated, "I wish you were more of a gentleman. Did you see the way Morris held the door for Mandy?" Dan snapped back, "Well, if you were as submissive as Mandy I would have picked you up and carried you into the house." Everything went downhill from there. They went back and forth saying harsh things to each other. Each complained about how the other did not measure up to their friends. The night ended with them both upset and, frankly, jealous over the seemingly perfect relationship that Morris and Mandy had. What they did not know was Morris and Mandy were attending marriage-counseling sessions every day of the week. They were simply doing the things that the marriage counselor had recommended to see if their marriage was worth saving.

Have you ever heard the saying "the grass isn't greener on the other side"? If you want your grass (marriage) to look nice and green, I recommend that you get some grass seeds (the word of God), water them (prayer), and let the sun (Jesus Christ) perfect his work in your marriage. It is never okay to try to make your spouse feel jealous of or less than someone else. You can look at other people's lives and marriages and become jealous of what you think they have. Instead of focusing on someone else's marriage, pray and ask God to show you what you need to do for your marriage to be what He designed it to be.

It is important to keep in mind that no marriage is perfect. Why? Because no one is perfect. Do not look at someone's marriage and allow jealousy to creep into your heart. Jealousy will not pull you towards your spouse; it will only push you away.

Love Note

Pray and ask God to show you what you need to do for your marriage to be what He designed it to be.

Prayer:

Father,

May I never compare my spouse to anyone. Help me to focus on making my marriage be all that you designed it to be. Show me any areas where I have allowed jealousy to creep in and that cause me to compare my spouse to anyone. In Jesus' name, I pray!

Amen!

Personal Notes

_____

_____

_____

_____

_____

_____

Day 7
Thankful Love
Love does not brag (boast)
-1 Corinthians 13:4

Lauryn was on the phone talking to her mom one evening when Larry walked in. He overheard her bragging about being a "superwoman" and having to do everything on her own. Lauryn recently had a baby and now it is time for her to return to work. Due to her shorter commute, and choosing to work part-time instead of full-time, the couple decided that she would drop off and pick up the baby from daycare. Lauryn also does the majority of the cooking and cleaning due to Larry's long workday. When Larry comes home he is often exhausted. Therefore, he eats, plays with the baby, and then gets ready for bed.

Lauryn finished talking to her mom and went to see how Larry's day had been. Larry stated he had a long exhausting day. Lauryn responded by saying she does not understand why he is always so tired. She pointed out that he does nothing around the house and proceeded to list all the things she does. Larry quickly reminded her that he took the job with the long commute not because he wanted to but because they needed the increase in pay for her to work part-time and to cover the baby's expenses. He also reminded her that he gets up in the middle of the night to change the diapers and to do the bottle feedings. That is in addition to waking up two hours before her every morning. The conversation quickly turned into a battle of who sacrifices the most. Larry was left feeling as if Lauryn does not see the contribution he makes to the family. He has grown tired of her always bragging about being able to do it "all on her own" while disregarding his many sacrifices.

Have you ever been guilty of overemphasizing all you do on a day-to-day basis while overlooking what your spouse does? Think about it. When you make a to do list, it normally includes all the things you have to get done, not what your spouse has to do. Nevertheless, it is important not to brag about all you do for your family. Your boasting (or playing the martyr) can make your spouse feel as though you do not value or recognize his or her contribution to your family.

Marriage requires sacrifice from both spouses. It is very easy to think about all you do and sacrifice. Try to take your eyes off you, and think about what your spouse does and has to sacrifice. Upon recognizing what your spouse does, begin to verbalize your appreciation and acknowledge your spouse's commitment to your marriage. Boasting about yourself and your contribution to the marriage does not make you look good, and it does not make your spouse feel good. So, when your spouse comes to you complaining about being tired, do not begin to talk about how you had way more to do, while dismissing your spouse's feelings.

Love Note

Boasting does not make you look good nor does it make your spouse feel good.

Prayer:

Father,

Help me see the role my spouse plays in my life. May I never forget to recognize the reason you placed them in my life to be my "helpmate". May I never get so caught up in myself that I forget about my spouse. May I never choose to boast in myself but only in your goodness and faithfulness. In Jesus' name, I pray.

Amen!

Personal Notes

_____

_____

_____

_____

_____

_____

Day 8
Supportive Love
(Love) *is not arrogant*
-1 Corinthians 13:4

Linda and Lyndon decided to take on an extracurricular activity together. They wanted to make their marriage stronger and thought that taking a class together would help them. They went back and forth between which classes to take and eventually decided on a dance class, neither of them had taken before. The couple began the lessons and Lyndon caught on quickly. Linda, however, struggled with learning the routine. She became discouraged and shared her frustrations with Lyndon. Instead of encouraging his wife and practicing with her at home, he asked her if she would be okay with him getting a new dance partner. He told her that she danced like she had two left feet, and if he took on a new partner he could become a better dancer. Lyndon proceeded to talk about how everyone in the class told him he was a natural-born dancer. He had become arrogant, thinking only of himself and his progress. He forgot about his wife and the reason they signed up for the class in the first place.

Have you and your spouse ever done something together, and you ended up doing much better than your spouse? Or have you watched your spouse struggle in an area that you excel? If so, did you take time to help, or did you gloat at the fact that you did better? If you are excelling in an area in which your spouse is struggling, do not abandon them; go help them. Do not allow arrogance to enter into your heart and cause you to forget the importance of building up your spouse.

You should not allow your success to puff you up to the point that you leave your spouse hanging. Humble yourself, and choose to be there to support your spouse, even if it impedes your own personal progress. Your spouse will find security and comfort in knowing that you will not abandon them.

Love Note

If you see yourself excelling in an area that your spouse is struggling, do not abandon them. Go help them.

Prayer:

Father,

May I be willing to use the gifts and talents that you have given me to help my spouse. May I never allow pride in my gifts and talents cause me to think more highly of myself than I should. May I always choose to support my spouse in any way that I can. In Jesus' name, I pray.

Amen!

Personal Notes

_____

_____

_____

_____

_____

_____

Day 9
Respectful Love
(Love) *does not act unbecomingly*
-1 Corinthians 13:5

Ken and his wife Kelly attended his company's Christmas party. Ken is a very conservative guy, while his wife Kelly is a free spirit, and likes to be the life of the party. Before arriving at the venue, Ken kindly asked Kelly not to be the center of attention. Kelly nodded in agreement. After all, this was his company's Christmas event. They arrived at the party and Ken began to introduce his wife to his co-workers. Kelly soon became bored with the conversations around her, so she excused herself and went to the open bar. She ended up having one too many drinks and found herself on the dance floor, dancing inappropriately with one of Ken's co-workers. Ken, embarrassed and angry, escorted Kelly off the dance floor and left the party early.

Have you ever been embarrassed by something your spouse said or did? Have you ever embarrassed your spouse and felt horrible about your words or actions afterwards? As a married couple, you must consider your actions both in private and especially in public settings. The way you act can either bring honor or shame to your spouse.

Her husband is known in the gates, when he sits among the elders of the land. Her husband also, praises her saying: "Many daughters have done nobly, but you excel them all." This proverb [31:23, 28b] shows us that what we do in private and public reflects our spouses. They too will be praised or put down based on our actions. If your spouse is more conservative than you, when you go to an event with them turn it down a notch. You do not have to be the life of every party. You do not have to have that second glass of wine that may cause you to act in a way that embarrasses your spouse. On the other hand, if your spouse is very outgoing and invites you some place, you can loosen up a bit. Choose not to sit in a corner all night acting like you do not want to be there. Now, you may not get out on the dance floor and dance the night away, but you can have small talk and work the room with your spouse.

Have you ever heard the phrase "opposites attract"? The reason you married your spouse could have something to do with your different personalities. While your differences can be attractive and even complementary, they do not give you permission to act in a way that would embarrass or even make your spouse uncomfortable. When out in public, make sure that you act in a way that will bring honor to your spouse, and vice versa.

Love Note

Even though you may have different personalities, it does not give you permission to act in a way that would embarrass or even make your spouse uncomfortable.

Prayer:

Father,

Do not let me forget how my actions, my words, and my decisions affect my spouse. Teach me how to live a life that is pleasing to you and will bring honor and not shame to my spouse. In Jesus' name, I pray.

Amen!

Personal Notes

_____

_____

_____

_____

_____

_____

Day 10
Sacrificial Love
(Love) *does not seek its own*
-1 Corinthians 13:5

Kima found herself in situations where she was constantly giving to everyone in her life but getting very little in return. When her sister would call, Kima would run to aide her; but her sister always had an excuse not to return the favor. The same was true with her friends and ex-boyfriends. Kima felt like no one was ever there for her when she was in need. She decided that from now on, she would only think about herself.

A couple years later, Kima met an awesome guy named Kyle, and they got married. Kyle was like no one she had ever met before. Kyle knew what she needed before she asked. Kima was confused; she was used to being mistreated and did not know how to respond to Kyle's attentiveness. She instinctively put her defenses up, fearing that when she needed him the most he would not be there. However, day after day, he proved her wrong. It became quite obvious that Kyle was not selfish and constantly thought about her needs. When her car broke down, he offered his car to her and woke up early to catch the bus until her car was repaired. When she wanted to start blogging, Kyle made sure she had all the resources needed to start. Kyle's selfless love won Kima over. Eventually, she began to put her guard down around him.

Have you ever felt as though you are constantly being taken advantage of? Have you felt like you are always there for everyone but when you need help no one is there for you? Such sentiments leave you feeling bitter and selfish. You cannot allow that bitterness and hurt from past experiences determine how you will treat your spouse. You cannot have this "I am going to look out for me and only me" mentality, especially in a marriage.

Love is willing to go out of its way with no expectation of gaining something in return. (Love was Jesus Christ dying on that cross not knowing who would or would not accept Him as their Lord and Savior.) That is our example of love. In a marriage, you should be willing to lay it all on the line. You should not be concerned whether your spouse will return the love, hugs, gifts, acts of service. You do it because that is what God requires of you.

Love Note
You cannot allow that bitterness and hurt from past experiences determine how you will treat your spouse.

Prayer:

Father,

Teach me how to love sincerely and how to love without putting requirements or expectations on my spouse to love me in return. May I not let the hurt I have dealt with in my past determine how I will treat my spouse. In Jesus' name, I pray.

Amen!

Personal Notes

_____

_____

_____

_____

_____

_____

Day 11
Covenant Love
(Love) *is not provoked*
-1 Corinthians 13:5

As Alex was preparing to go home from work, he replayed in his head the argument he had with his wife Andrea that morning. He went back and forth as to why he constantly allowed her to upset him. After-all, he recognizes what she is doing and yet continues to take the bait and argue with her. He is as disappointed with himself as he is with Andrea for constantly provoking him. Alex decided that he had to get to the root of why he was easily provoked. He was no longer going to treat his wife as the problem (even though she played a role) but take responsibility for his actions.

The more he replayed the argument, the more he realized that he would rather prove that he was right instead of showing the love of God. He did not want Andrea to think that she could continuously push his buttons and he would take it. He realized that his motives were wrong and decided to switch up his tactics. He understood that the only way he could stop Andrea from constantly provoking him was to love her. So, when Andrea came home from work in a bad mood, he decided he would ask her what happened at work and then sit there and listen. Some days it worked, other days it did not. However, Alex understood that how he responded to his wife's actions determined whether he would be provoked to anger or not.

Have you ever had an argument with your spouse in the morning and replayed it all day long in your head, thinking of "comeback statements" (what you should have said in response to their comments)? In that moment, did you plan out how to reconcile the relationship, or how to further provoke them so you could use those "come-backs" to make you feel like the victor. When having a disagreement with your spouse, your goal should be to resolve the issue, not perpetuate it with insults.

It does not matter if you have been married for a week or fifty years.

You have probably figured out what gets on your spouse's nerves. Unfortunately, these buttons can be pushed to provoke your spouse to anger, or even manipulate them. If your intention is to get what you want or to bring your spouse harm by provoking them, you are creating a problem.

Love Note
When having a disagreement with your spouse, your goal should be to resolve the issue, not perpetuate it.

Prayer:

Father,

Help me to take responsibility for the arguments that my spouse and I have. Show me ways to display the love of Christ in moments when I want to respond in anger. Teach me how to use my words to bring forth reconciliation instead of provoking my spouse to anger. I want my spouse to experience my love even when we are having a disagreement. May I always choose to love simply because that is what you require of me. In Jesus' name, I pray.

Amen!

Personal Notes

_____

_____

_____

_____

_____

_____

Day 12
Forgiving Love
(Love) *does not take into account a wrong suffered*
-1 Corinthians 13:5

Jan and Jim began dating in the ninth grade and got married right after high school. They decided to attend the same university and work part-time to pay for their off-campus apartment. Jan became a Biology major; Jim, a Sports Management major. Due to their busy schedules, they rarely saw each other. Jan started spending a lot of time in the lab with her lab partner. She often found herself flirting with him and enjoying their time together so much that they would catch a movie or go out to dinner. Jim was unaware of this relationship until he saw them leaving the lab one day, holding hands. Jim confronted Jan and demanded that she end it immediately. Jan told Jim that it was a harmless relationship, and she did not understand his anger or concern. However, she did end it.

The couple went to marriage counseling, where Jim eventually said that he could forgive Jan. Since then, whenever the two have a disagreement, Jim always reminds Jan of the incident. It's been five years, yet Jim will not let it go.

Do you tell your spouse that you forgive them, but you find yourself reminding them of their past mistakes? When you forgive someone, you treat him or her as though the incident never occurred. Constantly reminding them about the incident prevents both you and your spouse from healing and moving forward. Everyone makes mistakes and yes, you should address the reoccurring ones. However, if you choose to forgive make sure you truly forgive. In order to truly forgive you have to make a conscious decision to forget the past hurts caused by your spouse. You have the ability to control what you think, cast down any thoughts that would remind you of your spouse's past mistakes.

If you truly forgive your spouse, then your actions should align with your words. Do not hinder your growth or the growth of your spouse because of your unforgiving heart. Choose to humble yourself and think about all the wrong you have done and the time it took for people to forgive you. Most importantly, think about how many times you sin before God, and the many times He has had to forgive you. Love does not take into account wrongs suffered and neither should you.

Love Note
You have the ability to control what you think, cast down any thoughts that would remind you of your spouse's past mistakes.

Prayer:

Father,

May I never forget your example of dying on the cross for me so that my sins could be forgiven and my wrongs made right through the blood of the lamb. May I remember that you require me to forgive. May I not take on the character of Satan as the accuser of the brethren, always reminding my spouse of the wrongs committed. May I choose to forgive and forget because you do this for me. May I give my spouse the opportunity to change and no longer continue to throw their wrongs in their face. In Jesus' name, I pray.

Amen!

Personal Notes

_____

_____

_____

_____

_____

Day 13
Uplifting Love
(Love) does not rejoice in unrighteousness…
-1 Corinthians 13:6

Landon came to his wife Lila with what he thought was a great business idea. She has an MBA, and Landon thought that she would be the best person to guide him in starting up the business. After listening carefully to his idea, Lila concluded that it was not a good one. She also told him that, as a Christian, he should not go into an industry that promotes sin. He listened to her advice but decided he still wanted to proceed with the business despite her reservation and conviction.

Landon's business failed within the first three months of starting it. He knew that he should have listened to his wife; he knew that God was not pleased with his decision. He felt defeated and discouraged. Most of all, He was reluctant to tell Lila. He gathered up the nerves to tell her what happened, and she uttered the words he dreaded to hear - "I told you so!" - with a smirk. And with that, Landon felt worthless.

Have you ever told your spouse, "I told you so"? "I knew it wasn't going to work"? "If you had listened to me you wouldn't have failed"? How do you think your spouse felt after hearing those statements? Did you say anything to console them, or did you simply point out the obvious? Those words or thoughts should not be used when addressing your spouse after a failure. Your spouse knew what you said, so have some compassion. When your spouse chooses to ignore your advice, pray for them. Pray God's protection around them. Pray that they would consider your advice the next time you foresee a disaster. The point is, when your spouse fails and/or sins against God, do not use that as an opportunity to make your point. Instead of putting down your spouse or pointing out their sin (something they already know), you should be encouraging them to repent and not to give up.

Think about how many wrong decisions you have made, and how God was right there to shield you from destruction. When your spouse fails, that is when they need you the most. You need to be there and show love and support, not disappointment or excitement about you being right and them being wrong. Your words should be used to encourage them, not to tear them down.

Love Note
When your spouse fails at something, that is when they need you the most.

Prayer:

Father,

When my spouse decides to do things that I have warned them against help me not to rejoice in their failures. May I always stand for righteousness in my marriage and may I do it in a way that pleases you. Teach me how to pray so that my spouse can be protected from decisions that are not in alignment with your word or will. Teach me how to build them up and support them and not tear them down. In Jesus' name, I pray.

Amen!

Personal Notes

_____

_____

_____

_____

_____

_____

Day 14
Truthful Love
(Love) *rejoices with the truth*
-1 Corinthians 13:6

Melany has a problem. She gives away her money to others despite her own financial hardships. When she was single, it was just her problem. Now she is married, and it is beginning to be her husband's problem, too. Melany accumulated a serious amount of debt on a personal credit card due to her lending money that was never repaid. She knew that her husband Max would disapprove, so she hid it from him. He did not ask, so she did not tell. Melany paid the minimum balance in hopes of paying it off one day, but high interest rates made it impossible. She felt guilty and overwhelmed about keeping the debt a secret so she eventually told her husband.

Even though Max was upset about the debt, he was happy that she had confided in him. Melany felt as though a big weight had been lifted off her shoulders. Max and Melany discussed her inability to tell others no and the truth about her current financial position. They also came up with a plan for her to pay the debt off over the next couple of months.

Now, before you judge Melany, ask yourself how many shopping bags you have sneaked inside the house, praying that your spouse did not see them? Think about the numerous times when your spouse asked you about a new article of clothing or electronic device and you responded, "This old thing? I've had it for months," knowing you recently bought it. You may think these "little white lies" cannot hurt your marriage but they can. Before you know it, your spending can get out of control and, you have accumulated excessive amounts of debt.

Do not be in bondage because you are hiding things from your spouse. If you are struggling with something tell your spouse, they may have the solution. If not, you can work together to find one. Be honest, and remember that your spouse may be upset at first but will ultimately rejoice in the truth. So, do yourself a favor and tell the truth.

Love Note
If you are struggling with something tell your spouse, they may have the solution.

Father,

I thank you for your word. For your word is the truth that sets me free. Your truth allows me to be honest with my spouse no matter what situation I face. May I never hide the truth from my spouse, may I never be in bondage to living a lie. May your word, your truth concerning any situation that I face set me free. Thank you for allowing me to rejoice in your truth. In Jesus' name, I pray.

Amen!

Personal Notes

_____

_____

_____

_____

_____

_____

Day 15
Enduring Love
(Love) *bears all things, believes all things...*
-1 Corinthians 13:7

Joe and Joan have been married for 15 years. About six months ago, Joan lost her mom and fell into a deep depression. The depression prevented her from being able to work, or help with any household chores. Without any children or relatives nearby, Joe had no one to help him which left him feeling overwhelmed. Every morning Joe wakes up hoping that the Joan he knew before her mom died would return to him.

Lately, thoughts of leaving have slowly crept into his mind. He does not believe he can bear all the responsibility by himself. He does not want to be selfish and leave her alone, so he continues to endure and hope for the best.

Have you ever felt so overwhelmed by life that you just wanted to run away? Too often when things go wrong, giving up seems like the only solution. What do you do when your spouse does not have the strength to endure a hardship in life? What do you do when your spouse has lost all hope? Do you help them or do you leave to them?

Marriage is a huge challenge. Think about some of the challenges you have faced in your marriage. Did you consider leaving your spouse? When you stated your vows, you made a covenant to be with your spouse through sickness and health until death do you part. You probably could not imagine your spouse suffering from a sickness but when trials come to test your marriage you have to bear down and ask God to strengthen you. You do not abandon your spouse when they need you the most. There is more than one way to help, so pray and ask God how you should help.

Word of Love

If what your spouse is going through is putting your life in danger, go to a place where you are safe and offer help from there. Pray for your spouse and find resources that will help bring forth the healing they desperately need.

Love Note

When trials come to test your marriage, you have to bear down and ask God to strengthen you.

Prayer:

Father,

Help me to bear all things. May I never feel like giving up and leaving my marriage is the only solution. Help me to seek out counsel when needed. May I choose love and pray for my marriage. Help me to stay focused on the plan you have for my marriage and not my current situation. Prepare my heart to be solution driven and not divorce driven when obstacles occur. In Jesus' name, I pray.

Amen!

Personal Notes

_____

_____

_____

_____

_____

_____

Day 16
Hopeful Love
(Love) *hopes all things*
-1 Corinthians 13:7

For the past five years George and Georgia have tried to conceive a child. When they found out Georgia was pregnant, they knew without a doubt it was God answering their prayers. That was until Georgia had a miscarriage. The loss of the child has left them full of sorrow. There were moments when they were so full of anger that they could not console each other. They could not understand how God would allow them to conceive but not give birth to a child. Nevertheless, they said they would not turn away from God or each other. They decided to put their hope and trust in Him even though they did not understand.

George and Georgia sought counseling and continued to serve God while grieving the loss of their child. They had some good days and some really bad days, however, they chose to keep their hope in Christ. About two years later they conceived a child and eventually gave birth to that child. Even though they did not understand why they lost their first child they chose to believe that God would restore everything that was lost and He did.

Have you ever longed for something so badly, only to end up devastated? It is so easy to lose hope, especially after being disappointed over and over again. Losing hope can make you withdraw or push your spouse and God away. In moments of hurt and disappointment, make it a priority to show each other love like never before.

In moments of hopelessness, put your hope in the word of God and cleave to your spouse. God will restore all that has been lost. Keep the faith and keep showing each other love.

Love Notes

In moments of hurt and disappointment, make it a priority to show each other love like never before.

Prayer:

Father,

May I never lose hope in the plans you have for me, my marriage, or in you. Your word says that you know the plans you have for me, plans for welfare (good) and not for calamity (evil) to give me a future and a hope. May I grab hold of the hope and not let it go until it is manifested in my life. I will hope the best concerning my spouse. I will hope the best concerning my marriage. Thank you for giving me hope. In Jesus' name, I pray.

Amen!

Personal Notes

_____

_____

_____

_____

_____

_____

Day 17
Consistent Love
(Love) *endures all things*
-1 Corinthians 13:7

Tiara and Tim have been married for 9 years and separated for 11 months. According to state law, they could not get a divorce until they had been separated for one year. Tiara was counting down the days until she could legally file for a divorce. She had grown tired of the lies and was ready to move on with her life without Tim. One day as Tiara was praying to God she came across 1 Corinthians 13:7 and it said, *"love endures all things"*. Tiara began to reflect on why she wanted to get a divorce. She realized that the issues that seemed so big at the time were things that could be addressed with counseling. Tiara knew that she could not file for a divorce without doing everything she could to help reconcile her marriage. She decided to give her marriage another chance and it started with counseling to help her deal with the hurt she felt in her marriage. Once she completed one-on-one counseling she went to marriage counseling with Tim. They are now living together and working on rebuilding their trust in each other. They have a lot of work to do but they are working hard to restore their marriage. Every time Tiara faces adversity and wants to give up she remembers that *love endures all things*.

Do you envision your life being easier if you were not married? When your marriage is facing adversity do you automatically think "I need to get a divorce", or do you say, "how can we make this marriage work"? Disagreements and disappointments are going to happen in your marriage, but they do not have to ruin your marriage. You must be prepared to endure life with your spouse through the good and the bad.

Endurance requires consistent training, so you must be consistent in your effort to love. Make your words, thoughts, and actions align with what you are believing God for. Find a scripture and memorize it so you can be encouraged when times get hard. John 20:29 states

Blessed are they who did not see, and yet they believed. When moments of doubt or frustration arise, are you going to choose to believe God's word over your reality? Choose to endure through it all knowing that God will work it out for your good.

Love Note
Endurance requires consistent training, so you must be consistent in your effort to love.

Prayer:

Father,

Teach me how to endure, how to push my emotions aside and be consistent in my words, thoughts, and actions. May I be the example of consistency in my marriage just like you are in my life. You are the same yesterday, today, and forever. Thank you for renewing my strength so that I will not grow weary and quit, but I will continue to endure. In Jesus' name, I pray.

Amen!

Personal Notes

_____

_____

_____

_____

_____

_____

Victorious Love

Love never fails
-1 Corinthians 13:8

As a result of feeling neglected by her husband Joseph, Justine made a very poor decision. She cheated on him. It was not something she planned on doing and she was very ashamed. Her husband was a workaholic, and he told Justine multiple times that he enjoyed working far more than spending time with her. One day Justine met a seemingly amazing guy at a coffee shop. This man made her feel like she was the only woman in the world. They would have long talks about everything, and he noticed every little detail about her (something she felt her husband had never done). Justine looked forward to meeting him daily at the coffee shop. She loved the attention he gave her. Months later she found herself committing adultery and even starting to fall in love with this other man.

Eventually, Joseph found out about her infidelity and confronted her. She told him the truth and he decided to divorce her. Justine tried apologizing and explaining how the adultery happened but Joseph would not listen to her. Joseph was angry at the thought of his wife being with someone else. He loved her even though he had done a poor job showing it. A part of him wanted to stay and work it out but his pride and anger towards her prevented him from doing so. Justine was in complete disbelief that Joseph would not give her a second chance. After all, she felt as though he was the reason she cheated. If he had spent more time with her she would not have taken interest in another person. She could not understand how Joseph blamed her for the marriage failing when she thought his lack of attention towards her was the cause?

Justine left the marriage with so much hurt, she decided to seek counsel. With the help of a counselor, Justine was able to accept her part in her marriage failing. It was through counseling that Justine realized that she had turned to another man instead of turning to God to fill the gap in her marriage. She was repenting repentful for her actions and spent the next couple of years cultivating a relationship with Christ. She did not want to enter into another relationship until she was healed from the previous one. About five years later, Justine bumped into Joseph. They had a really good conversation which resulted in them both apologizing for their part in the marriage failing. They decided to meet up the following day and the rest is history. Here they are a year later planning their second wedding.

Have you ever felt neglected by your spouse? Have you felt like a job, friends, family, children, or a hobby was more important to your spouse than you? How you address this issue can cause your marriage to fail or succeed. Your spouse can fail you in various ways but God can never fail you. God desires to be your all, for He is the only one who can meet all your needs. God wants to be your first choice, your first love. God wants to hear your concerns. He wants you to trust him with your marriage. God wants you to know that He will never leave you nor forsake you and that His love never fails. Open the word of God and allow it to guide you. Allow God's love for you to cause you to pray for your spouse and for your marriage.

Without Christ, you do not have the ability to love like God. You must allow Him to teach you how to love. Love is a decision and you have to decide that you are going to love even when you do not feel like it. Be the example of love in your household for your spouse, for your marriage, for your family, and for your future bloodline.

Love Note

Love is a decision and you have to decide that you are going to love even when you do not feel like it.

Prayer:

Father,

Thank you that your love does not fail. There is nothing about your love that gives up, or that does not accomplish the task. Your love wins, and because your love wins and your love abides in me - I WIN. My marriage wins, and my family wins. I thank you for being the very example of what love is. As I desire to love like you, help me. In Jesus' name, I pray.

Amen!

Personal Notes

_____

_____

_____

_____

_____

_____

Day 19
Unified Love
...any city or house divided against itself will not stand.
-Matthew 12:25

Asia and Andrew are at a point in their marriage where they feel as though they are no longer compatible. The two cannot find any common ground. They married each other due to the fact that they were so different from each other and they found each other interesting. Asia is a Christian and Andrew has no interest in religion. Asia likes to save money and Andrew likes to spend money. Asia is a health nut and Andrew does not know the last time he ate something green or exercised. Their inability to agree on most things has caused major turmoil in their marriage, especially when it comes to addressing topics such as raising children. Asia wants her children to attend church and a Christian school and Andrew believes the children should be able to make their own choice about religion and education. This is one of their many conflicts. Due to their inability to agree on things they have not accomplished much in their marriage.

In order to have a successful marriage you cannot be divided on the important things. It is very important for you to develop a plan for your family; develop some family goals. For example, if you desire to have kids talk about how many you want, how you are going to discipline them, how you want to educate them, etc. It is also important to make sure that you have conversations about finances. You should set goals that both people can achieve. One spouse should not dictate to the other where money can and cannot be spent. On the other hand, one spouse should not drive the other into debt because of poor spending habits. The point is you must be on one accord and in agreement on things that will have an impact on both of your lives (that is practically everything). Having these conversations could prevent you from marrying someone who has different values than you. In a marriage, there is no room for division. It will only drive you apart, and you will soon feel like you are incompatible or forget the very reason you got married.

Word of Love

Pre-marital counseling is very important in marriage. It helps you discuss issues you may not have thought of. This allows you to see if you both value the same thing. If you were not able to get pre-marital counseling do not worry. It is not too late for you to seek counseling if need be.

Love Note

In order to have a successful marriage, you cannot be divided.

Prayer:

Father,

May we take time to communicate about the issues of life. May we take time to plan and set goals in place, so we can be successful in our marriage. Father, help us to see our future the way that you see it. May our plans not be set in stone, but may they be open to whatever you have in mind for us. May we be a house that is united not one that is divided. In Jesus' name, I pray.

Amen!

Personal Notes

_____

_____

_____

_____

_____

_____

Day 20
Intimate Love

The husband must fulfill his duty to his wife, and likewise also the wife to her husband. The wife does not have authority over her own body, but the husband does; and likewise also the husband does not have authority over his own body, but the wife does. Stop depriving one another, except by agreement for a time, so that you may devote yourselves to prayer, and come together again so that Satan will not tempt you because of your lack of self-control.
-1 Corinthians 7:3-5

Vinny is frustrated with his wife Vanessa. He is tired of making sexual advancements and being turned down. The only time Vanessa pursues him is when she wants something; other than that, she could care less if they had sex. Vanessa views sex as a way to reward Vinny when he does something that pleases her. Recently, Vinny stopped trying to be intimate with his wife. Vanessa noticed that he has not pursued her in months and now thoughts of him committing adultery are starting to creep into her mind.

Do you use sex like a merit based program? I will have sex with you if you have done something to make me think you deserve it. Or maybe you withhold sex if your spouse does something that displeases you. If so, you should know that sex was not created so that you could dominate or manipulate your spouse. It was created so that you could cherish and serve the person you are married to in the bedroom or wherever you prefer (except in public places you could go to jail).

The second you say, "I do" your body now belongs to your spouse. The scripture at the beginning of today's devotional clearly states that you do *not have authority over your body* it belongs to your spouse. So, wives stop faking those headaches or pretending that you are sleep because you do not feel like having sex. Sex should not be done with the intention of getting what you want, whether it be a new pair of shoes or a child. Husbands stop acting like you cannot go one day without sex. If you know your wife is exhausted let her sleep and help lighten her load. Do not wake her up in the middle of the night without her permission to meet your needs. Sex should not be used to make your wife your sex slave. It should be used as a way to show her the love you have for her.

Sex in a marriage is a way to serve your spouse, to please your spouse, and that should be your top priority. It is your responsibility to cherish and serve the person you are married to; that includes in the bedroom. I urge you to be aware of this verse "Stop depriving one another, except by agreement for a time, so that you may devote yourselves to prayer, and come together again so that Satan will not tempt you because of your lack of self-control." The last thing you want in a marriage is for your spouse to be tempted to find sex or affection of any kind elsewhere. So, do not be selfish with your body, realize that it is no longer yours and trust your spouse to love it and please it.

Love Note

It is your responsibility to cherish and serve the person you are married to; that includes in the bedroom.

Prayer:

Father,

Wipe away all of my preconceived ideas about sex and show me your heart concerning it. Turn my heart toward wanting to please my spouse. May I truly give my body to my spouse and trust it will be loved the way you desire it to be. If there are any areas in my life preventing me from being able to do this, show me what they are and bring forth healing in those areas. Thank you Lord for protecting my marriage and turning my heart away from any temptation that could destroy it. In Jesus' name, I pray!

Amen!

Personal Notes

_____

_____

_____

_____

_____

_____

Day 21
Protective Love

The eye is the lamp of the body. If your eyes are good, your whole body will be full of light. But if your eyes are bad, your whole body will be full of darkness. If then the light within you is darkness, how great is that darkness!
-Matthew 6:22-23 (NKJV)

Christine's husband Chris enjoys going to strip clubs. He does not spend a lot of money; he just goes there to look. When they first married Christine did not see a problem with his going; after all, he is "just looking". Later on, she noticed an increase in their cable bill; inquired about it, and found that her husband had been purchasing tons of pornography. Now, Chris is frequenting the strip clubs a lot more and has become disinterested in his wife. Christine is now left battling feelings of insecurity and feels as though pornography and strip clubs have replaced her. She has accepted that her husband has a problem and he needs help in order for their marriage to have a chance. She often blames herself because she encouraged him to start going to the strip clubs with his friends never thinking that it could destroy their marriage.

Have you ever heard the saying "you can look but do not touch?" Do not believe those words. The Bible states in Matthew 5:28 that *anyone who looks at a woman lustfully has already committed adultery with her in his heart*. So, if you look, you have already committed a sin against God. Sin that is not dealt with through repentance leads to more sin. Eventually, you may not just look; you might touch.

You must choose to protect your spouse, and your marriage. Looking can plant a seed for infidelity; you must protect your eyes. The word of God says in Matthew 6:22 that *the eye is the lamp to the body*. It is important that you protect your eyes and heart, by choosing not to look at someone lustfully. Make your spouse your one and only standard for beauty and sexiness. You do not want your eyes to be subjected to sin. So, if that means putting down the magazine, turning off the television or not going to the mall then do it. Your marriage is worth the sacrifice. You do not want your marriage to unfold because sin is reigning in your hearts all because you decided to look.

Love Note
Make your spouse your one and only standard for beauty and sexiness.

Prayer:

Father,

I keep me away from lust, thank you for always showing me the way to stay away and escape from it. I pray protection over my eyes to keep them from sinning. Help me to stay focused on pleasing you. May I not lead my spouse down the road to destruction by allowing them to believe that it is okay to "look as long as they don't touch". May they desire only me and I desire only them. Thank you, God for the marriage covenant, protect it with the blood of Jesus. In Jesus' name, I pray!

Amen!

Personal Notes

_____

_____

_____

_____

_____

_____

Day 22
Obedient Love

In the same way, you wives be submissive to your own husbands so that even if any of them are disobedient to the word, they may be won without a word by the behavior of their wives, as they observe your chaste and respectful behavior.
-1 Peter 3:1

Edward and Evelyn have been married almost five years. When they first got married, Edward would accompany Evelyn to church every Sunday. Two years into the marriage Edward's church attendance began to decrease; he would go one or two Sundays out of the month. If it was football season his attendance decreased even more. In addition to his low church attendance Evelyn noticed that Edward no longer reads his bible or prays. This bothers Evelyn because those were the things that attracted her to him. She decided to ask Edward why he no longer attended church or read his bible and he said, "his relationship with God was between him and God and no one else". Evelyn began to nag Edward about going to church and would make comments like "I would not have married you if I knew you were not going to go to church". Eventually she even questioned Edward about his salvation. She could not understand why he made these changes, and wondered if he only did these things in the beginning of the relationship to please her. Evelyn became concerned about the future of her marriage. One day she was reading her bible and came across 1 Peter 3:1. It reminded her of her responsibility to live a life that glorified the God she served. Edward still does not attend church with Evelyn, but she has decided to pray for Edward and let God work on his heart.

Has your spouse stopped attending church, reading the bible or praying with you? Have you noticed a decline in your spouse's spiritual walk and it concerns you? Guess what, 1 Peter 3:1 reveals that there is more power in submission than there is in nagging, grumbling, and complaining about the issue. Your actions, your obedience, and your willingness to be respectful to your spouse can help bring forth the change you want to see in your spouse. Stop quoting scripture to them, or blasting Christian music through the house in hopes of forcing them to change. You cannot change your spouse only God can do that. However, you can influence them by living a godly life before them and that starts with submission. If your spouse is not a Christian; if they do not have a personal relationship with Jesus Christ there is a way to lead your spouse to Christ without condemnation. You do not have to express your disappointment or constantly nag your spouse to go to church with you. Your submission to Christ, your obedience to the word of God is what will make salvation and obedience desirable.

Love Note

Your actions, your obedience, and your willingness to be respectful to your spouse can help you bring forth the change you want to see in your spouse.

Prayer:

Father,

Thank you for showing me that there is power in submission; there is power in being obedient to your word. Father, may I continue to live a life submitted to you so that my marriage can prosper. Thank you for showing me that it is not my words that lead my spouse to change, but it is my submission unto you and my spouse that will bring forth change. In Jesus' name, I pray.

Amen!

Personal Notes

_____

_____

_____

_____

_____

_____

Day 23
Unmerited Love

He who finds a wife finds a good thing and obtains favor from the Lord.
-Proverbs 18:22

Roy lived a pretty good life, he was a manager at a local department store, he just recently bought a house and now he was ready for a family. He did not want just any woman, he wanted "The Woman". The woman that he could laugh with and trust; one he could build his dream life with. One day Roy was called to the customer service desk to help a customer, and that is where he met Rose. Her beautiful smile knocked him off his feet. He wanted to make sure she was extremely satisfied with the service he provided. After completing the transaction, Roy gathered up the nerve to ask Rose out on a date, which she gladly accepted. They dated for a year, and the more Roy got to know her the more he realized she had all the character traits he was looking for and more. Rose was an ambitious and adventurous woman. Roy wanted to know the reason behind her ambition; being around her made him want to be a better person. The more he got to know her the more he saw that her strengths relied heavily on her faith in her Lord and Savior Jesus Christ. Roy began to attend church with Rose and soon found himself accepting Jesus Christ as his Lord and Savior. Roy and Rose married the next year. Roy knew that God had favored him when He brought Rose into his store that day. Roy had a new wife and a Savior who made him feel like he could conquer the world.

Wives you should not have to remind your husband that you are the source of His favor. Your presence alone should be a reminder of what you are in his life. The word of God says when a man finds a wife he obtains favor from the Lord, not when a man marries a woman. A wife is someone who brings value to her husband. She understands her worth and knows the source of it is God.
Your spouse should experience favor because you are praying for them, encouraging them, and supporting them. As a married couple, you should push each other to be your best. So, husbands and wives do not take your "good thing" for granted. Treasure each other and

rejoice in all great things you will be able to accomplish together. Decide to enjoy your marriage, to find the good things in each other and about each other and focus on them. Though favor comes from God you can always make your spouse feel favored by loving, supporting, and encouraging them throughout life.

Love Note
Your spouse should experience favor because you are praying for them, encouraging them, and supporting them.

Prayer:

Father,

Remind me of the very reason I said, "I do". Remind me that my marriage is not always about my happiness but rather about bringing happiness to my spouse. Help me to always see the good things in my spouse. May we make marriage look desirable, because we want to honor you. May we always favor each other by being the best support system that we can be. I thank you God for your favor on our marriage. In Jesus' name, I pray.

Amen!

Personal Notes

_____

_____

_____

_____

_____

_____

Day 24
Peaceful Love

It is better to live in a corner of a roof, than in a house with a contentious (quarrelsome) woman.
-Proverbs 21:9

Shawn and his wife Shauna have been married for three years, and for three years Shawn has been in search for peace. He has read various books on marriage and attended multiple marriage seminars. However, he has yet to figure out what to do so that he and his wife can live in peace. Shauna is a very argumentative person; no matter what Shawn does she always finds something to argue about. For example, Shauna was complaining about the house being unorganized. One day while Shauna was at work Shawn stayed home and organized the house. When Shauna came home she immediately began to argue with Shawn because her belongings were not where she left them. Shawn has grown weary, and he feels as though he will never be able to live in peace with his wife. It has gotten so bad that he no longer wants to be in her presence. If she is in one room he goes to another in hopes of finding peace and refuge there.

Do you find yourself constantly disgruntled about something? Have you noticed that your spouse spends majority of their time in a different room than you? If so, you could be that contentious person mentioned above. Though this scripture specifically identifies a woman; no matter your gender it is not okay to be a quarrelsome person. If your spouse would rather live in the corner of a roof than in your house that is a problem. Your spouse would rather get rained on, snowed on, or sun burnt, than to live in a house with you.

Excuses can no longer be made to justify being quarrelsome and mean towards your spouse. You have to take responsibility for your actions or words. Your spouse cannot make you behave a certain way. Yes, your spouse can provoke you to anger, but ultimately you choose how you respond. It is the sin in your precious little heart that causes you to show anything other than the love of God. There is a problem and if you look in the mirror you will see it. Decide to grab ahold of those emotions that cause you to say, do, and react any other way than what Christ would expect from you. Ask the Lord to show you how to be a peacemaker. Your marriage will be better because of it.

Love Note
Excuses can no longer be made to justify being quarrelsome and mean towards your spouse.

Prayer:

Father,

Help me learn how to control my emotions. May my spouse not view me as overbearing, or quarrelsome. May they want to come home to me knowing that I am there to love and encourage them. May my home be a place where peace dwells. May I live a peaceful life that causes my spouse to want to be around me. Show me effective ways to communicate with my spouse. In Jesus' name, I pray.

Amen!

Personal Notes

_____

_____

_____

_____

_____

Day 25
One Love

For this reason man shall leave his father and his mother, and be joined to his wife; and they shall become one flesh.
-Genesis 2:24

November has arrived and Malica discussed with her husband Malik the desire to have Thanksgiving dinner at their new home. Malica knew that her mother-in-law normally cooked a huge family dinner and she expected all of her children to be there. Therefore, Malica informed her mother- in-law of her plans and invited her to dinner. She also invited some of her immediate family and a few close friends. A week before Thanksgiving Malica was going to the grocery store so she asked her husband Malik what Thanksgiving dishes he would prefer. Malik stated, "there is no need for you to cook; we are going to my mom's for Thanksgiving like we have done in the past". Malica was angry. She told Malik that she had spoken to his mom, and informed her about her Thanksgiving plans at the beginning of the month. Malik told his wife that she could proceed with her plans but he was going to his moms. Malica began to express her desire to start her own family traditions, and how tired she was of his mom having the final say in their lives. However, Malik never changed his stance he was going to his moms.

This was not the first disagreement they had regarding his Mom. His mom comes over whenever she wants without calling ahead of time, she plans their vacations to ensure she is included, and has even talked to them about when to start having children. Malik is a "mama's boy", he cannot tell her no. He would rather disappoint his wife than disappoint his mom. Malica feels as though she is in constant competition with her mother in-law for her husband's time, loyalty and love and is starting to feel like she is losing.

In-laws can be one of the most difficult challenges in a marriage. A lot of things have to change when you get married and some families have a hard time adjusting. As a married couple, you have to be willing to set boundaries and establish a new life together. Your parents can no longer expect you to spend every holiday with them, nor can they expect you to disregard your spouse's feelings and concerns to appease them. This does not mean you cannot include your family in your new life. It means you do not allow your family to control your new life.

There comes a time when you have to decide to leave your family and cleave to your spouse. You have to create new traditions and accept the responsibility of taking care of one another. You have to leave your parents and cleave to your spouse.

Love Note

As a married couple, you have to be willing to set boundaries and establish a new life together.

Prayer:

Father,

Show me what it really means to leave and cleave to my spouse. May I put my spouse and our marriage first. May we learn how to set boundaries in our marriage while not excluding our parents or other family members. May our families respect our union and encourage us to cleave to one another. In Jesus' name, I pray.

Amen!

Personal Notes

_____

_____

_____

_____

_____

_____

Day 26
Friendly Love
A man who has friends must himself be friendly…
-Proverbs 18:24 (NKJV)

Dan was taking his wife Deborah to meet up with her friends for a Saturday brunch. As he was dropping her off her friends approached the car and began to tell him how blessed he was to be married to Deborah. They went on to say how she brings so much laughter and adventure into their lives. Dan sat there puzzled wondering whose wife they were referring to. At home Deborah almost never laughs; she always seems so serious and stressed. Dan smiled and then left Deborah to be with her friends.

Once Deborah returned home Dan asked her if she was happy being married to him. He could not understand why he had not experienced this person that her friends described. Deborah began to explain to Dan that majority of their conversations involved work, finances, and what was going wrong in their marriage. She continued to explain to him that spending time with her friends allowed her to be herself and "let down her hair". While with her friends she was not concerned about work, money or marital issues. Dan was unaware that Deborah felt this way, but as he reflected on their conversations he began to understand her point of view. He decided that they had to find something they could do together that would help them enjoy each other more. Dan knew that he wanted to experience Deborah the way her friends did. He also knew that building a friendship was going to take time so he did not waste any time getting started.

Are you and your spouse friends? Do you have a hobby or something that you do together that causes you to relax and de-stress together? Do you get to experience a joyful and fun spouse or do you get to experience the disgruntled, stressed out spouse?

In marriage, you have so many roles to fulfill such as husband and wife, brother and sister in Christ, parents, lovers, and sometimes business partners/co-workers. These roles can prevent you from taking time to cultivate a friendship. Your spouse can be the very source of your stress and thus making them the last person that you want to be friends with. Who wants to go hang-out with the person they perceive to be the root of all their stress? So how do you cultivate a friendship within your marriage. Well you can start by being friendly; smile, laugh, flirt, tell silly jokes. You can also find something that you both enjoy doing and do it together. Be intentional about building your friendship and enjoying the time that you have together. Lastly, choose a time to discuss stressful, serious things and make sure it is not while you are out having fun.

Love Note
Be intentional about building your friendship and enjoying the time that you have together.

Prayer:

Father,

Show me how to be a friend to my spouse. Help me to find something that I enjoy doing with my spouse so that we can build a strong friendship. I want to experience all of my spouse and that includes having a friendship. In Jesus' name, I pray.

Amen!

Personal Notes

_____

_____

_____

_____

_____

_____

Day 27
Sincere Love
Love must be sincere...
-Romans 12:9 (NIV)

Sandra worked a twelve-hour shift without lunch, rushed to pick the kids up from daycare, went home to cook dinner, and feed the kids. As she was about to sit down her husband Sam asked her to fix him a dinner plate. She grumbled under her breath "he should be fixing my plate after all I have done today", all while practically throwing the plate at him. Sam did not know whether to eat the food or run for his life. It became obvious that his wife did not want to fix his plate. Later that evening Sandra asked Sam to take out the trash just as he was about to sit down and watch his favorite team play. He yelled "sure honey", but mumbled to himself "I know she saw me about to sit down and enjoy the game". Both Sandra and Sam did what was asked of them but neither did it sincerely.

Has your spouse ever asked you to do something when you were completely exhausted or when you were in the middle of doing something you enjoy. How did you respond, did you do it begrudgingly? If so, think about the message you sent to your spouse. One way to show your love is through your actions. If you do things begrudgingly it will be obvious. When it is done sincerely, it is done to your best ability and without complaint. When you do it begrudgingly, it may or may not be done correctly and it is most likely done with a complaint. Take some time and think about what you do for your spouse and ponder on your thoughts and attitude behind it. Could you say that you love your spouse based off the sincerity of your actions? The truth is sincerity matters. You want your spouse to do the things you ask of them with a joyful heart not a complaining mouth.

Love Note

One way to show your love is through your actions.

Prayer:

Father,

Thank you for showing me what sincere love looks like. The fact that you did not complain about having to sacrifice your son for me shows me that love can be sincere. Please remind me that I should do all things with a sincere heart. Father, show me the areas in which my love is not sincere. May, I repent and ask you to make my heart pure and clean. In Jesus' name, I pray.

Amen!

Personal Notes

_____

_____

_____

_____

_____

_____

Day 28
Valuable Love

An excellent wife, who can find? For her worth is far above jewels.
-Proverbs 31:10

Today, if you met Ari you would probably think she is a great
example of the Proverbs 31 woman because of the pride she takes in
being a homemaker. However, she has not always been that way. Ari
was not a homemaker by choice; she could not find a job in the city in
which she had recently moved. This new role as a homemaker has
been very challenging because she prided herself on being an
independent hardworking woman. She loved to work, she equated
her worth to her ability to provide for herself financially. Due to the
rural area in which she now lived she was no longer able to work.
One day, she told her husband Austin about the internal battle she
was having with her role as a homemaker. He gently stated to her
"The Word of God says *your worth is far above jewels and I agree*. I want
you to know that you bring tremendous value to our household".
Those kind words propelled her to study Proverbs 31 and she choose
to make that scripture the standard for the way she operated their
household.

Have you ever questioned if you brought value to your marriage?
Things can happen like the loss of a job and make you feel as though
you are being more of a burden than a help to your spouse. In those
moments, you must remember that your worth (who you are, not
what you do) brings value to your marriage. So, no matter what life
brings your way remember who you are. Do not allow money or your
ability to earn money to determine your value.

In Proverbs 31: 11-31 it continues to say how the husband trusts his
wife, and she does him good and not evil. The woman referenced in
the scriptures pursued excellence. She worked with her hands and her
heart. She had the ability to make wise decisions with their income
and she ensured that her families clothes were clean and in good
condition. Study this woman and see what you can learn from her.
How can you become as valuable in your household as she was in

hers? Your situation may look different than hers but your character can match up perfectly.

Love Note

You must remember that your worth (who you are, not what you do) brings value to your marriage.

Prayer:

Father,

Remind me how valuable I am in your sight. May I not take lightly any role that you have given especially when it pertains to my marriage. May I take the time to invest in myself, and in my family. May I desire to be excellent in all that I do. Show me ways that I can help add value to our family. In Jesus' name, I pray.

Amen!

Personal Notes

_____

_____

_____

_____

_____

_____

Day 29
Responsible Love

For the husband is the head of the wife, as Christ also is the head of the church. He Himself being the Savior of the body.
-Ephesians 5:23

Tony was a bit of a chauvinist. He did not consider Tayla's feelings or thoughts about anything. After all he was the "head of the household". What he said went, and she was to obey him. Tayla was a very passive woman. She never stood up for herself. She often prayed that God would strengthen her and show Tony the error of his ways.

One day Tony's friend Oscar was over and Tony began yelling commands at his wife. Oscar waited until Tayla left the room, and he confronted his friend. He simply stated that he did not think the way he was talking to his wife was honorable. He went on to say that he thought it was demeaning, and it made Tony look like less of a man. What a slap in the face. Tony thought that he looked like a man in charge because his wife was doing whatever he said. However, his friend saw it the opposite way. Oscar left Tony with a scripture, Ephesians 5:23. As Tony began to read it, he realized that he was wrong. Wrong for the way he treated his wife, and wrong for the way he thought about his role as a husband. He quickly asked his wife for forgiveness and never spoke to her in that way again.

Ephesians 5:23 speaks specifically about the role of a husband as the head of the household, which is a very important role. Without your head, you would not be able to function at all. The role of the husband is to be to the head of his wife. He seeks the Lord on how his household should function. He sees what lies ahead in the future for his family. He writes a vision for his family. He listens for the voice of God and moves accordingly. This is not a role to be taken lightly.

Have you said, "I'm the head", but have not fulfilled the position in the way that pleases God? The "head" is not just a title; it is a role.

This role requires very thoughtful actions for it is a position of service. The role as the "head" helps shape the future of your family. Seek the Lord regarding how to function in this role. Ask him for wisdom concerning any decisions you have to make. Wives, pray for your husband and speak life over your him. Give him sound advice when needed, while also leaving room for him to grow into his position as the head of your family.

Love Note
The role as the "head" helps shape the future of your family.

Prayer for husbands:

Father,

You made man head over his wife. You established order so that your children may function properly. Give me the confidence I need to fulfill this role. Give me the desire to seek out your wisdom and guidance for our family. May I never take for granted or take advantage of the position that you have given me in my family. In Jesus' name, I pray.

Amen!

Personal Notes

_____

_____

_____

_____

_____

_____

Day 30
Perfect Love

There is no fear in love; but perfect love casts out fear, because fear involves punishment, and the one who fears is not perfected in love.
-1 John 4:18-19

As a teenager Will witnessed the heart-wrenching divorce of his parents. It was then that he decided he would never get married. Years went by, and he had many promising relationships but he could never make that final commitment. Eventually, the ladies walked out of his life. While shopping, Will met Whitney. It was love at first site. They dated for over two years, and then one-day Whitney told him he had to make a decision about their future. He had to decide whether he would get over the fear of divorce and ask for her hand in marriage or move on without her. Will went back and forth about what he should do. On one hand, he vowed to never get married. He knew firsthand what divorce could do to a person, but he did not want to lose Whitney. He was full of fear. He thought his marriage would fail just like his parents.

Will decided to seek counsel from his best friend, Micah. Micah opened the bible and read 1 John 4:18-19 to him. Micah reminded Will that the choices his parents made did not determine his future. He reminded Will of the power of God's love that dwells inside of him. He assured him that God's power will help him have a lifelong marriage. A week later Will showed up at Whitney's door and got down on one knee and asked her to marry him.

Do you have fears that are hindering you from being all that God created you to be? Maybe you are afraid to give your marriage your "all", in fear of your heart being broken. Perhaps you are afraid to get rid of that "just in case fund" your spouse does not know about because you were taught to always have a backup plan. No matter the fear choose to let love fight the battle. Allow the love of God to come into your heart and uproot any fear that could hinder you as a person and/or harm your marriage.

God's love will protect you and His love will cause you to succeed and not fail. Decide today to let love drive your decisions and actions by taking away the power that fear has. There is freedom in love, decide today to embrace that freedom by putting your trust in the love of the Almighty God.

Love Note
God's love will protect you and His love will cause you to succeed and not fail.

Prayer:

Father,

Your word says that perfect love casts out fear. May your love be perfected in me and drive out all of my fears. Show me where I have allowed fear to rule my decisions and actions in my marriage and in my life. May I take the keys of love and break free from the bondage that fear once had over me. Father, you have forgiven me for all my sins, so may the fear of my past, or of future decisions no longer burden me. I thank you for the perfected love of Jesus Christ, and I choose to allow your love to be perfected in me. In Jesus' name, I pray.

Amen!

Personal Notes

_____

_____

_____

_____

_____

_____

Dedication

This devotional would not have been possible without the support of my awesome husband Malcom. Thank you for being honest with me even when I did not want to hear it. Your truthfulness and helpfulness aided me in completing this devotional. You are a wonderful provider, protector, priest and friend. I thank God for your patience, wisdom, and love. Stepping into the marriage ring with you has been one of the best decisions of my life. Marriage brings many challenges and instead of fighting against me you fought with me. It is my prayer that we will continue to knock out everything that comes to destroy our marriage. May we continue to learn new ways to love each other and may our marriage grow stronger every year. I love you and I am honored to serve in this marriage with you.

Acknowledgements

I could not have completed this devotional without the love, support, and input of my friends and family. There are so many people who have encouraged me to write this devotional. Words cannot express the gratitude or love I have for each one. So, I will simply say thank you. Thank you for brainstorming with me, praying for me, holding me accountable, and encouraging me to finish strong. There were so many times that I wanted to quit, but because of you all and God I continued to persevere.

To my parents, William (Caroletta), and Tonya thanks for making me feel loved and entrusting my husband with the responsibility to continue to do so. You have always made me feel like I could do anything and this book is a reflection of that.

To my father and mother in-law Malcom and Deborah, God really blessed me with you two. I could not have prayed for better in-laws. You make me feel so loved. Thank you for everything.

To my siblings, Apollonia (Antoine), Brittney (Travis), William, Emmit, and Debranetta (Al). Thanks for your constant support and resources to help me write this book. I love you all.

To my friends Stephanie, Janiya, Keoda, Tiffany C., April, Shania, LaToya, Tiffany S., Felecia, Jemale, Alicia, Kenyia, Mary, Joetta, Brandon, Lanisha, Allison, Shanel, Tier-ra, Dorine, Pastor Gail, and Simeaka thank you so much! You have encouraged me throughout this entire process. God has blessed me with some amazing friends and I am so grateful. Thank you!

To John, Michelle, Eric and Kim, Ms. Sharon, Aunt Lillie Wilson thank you for your support and review of this devotional. I appreciate your time and feedback. Blessings to you all.

To Terwana, thank you for helping me bring this book to fruition. I know I changed my format so many times and yet you remained patient and helped me finish strong. I appreciate you.

Lastly, to my dear sweet Malachi and Makayla. Mommy loves you so much. Thank you for your understanding when Mommy had to hide in the room to write or edit this book. I love you both and I am praying for your future spouses. May they be all that God desires them to be to help you fulfill your purpose in marriage.

Bio

Author, Laura T. Gethers is the dedicated wife of an awesome husband and home-schooling mother of their two amazing children.

Laura is the owner of Love Harder Marriage Coaching, LLC which is designed to equip married couples with tools to help strengthen their hearts so that their marriage can win. Love Harder hosts as well as partners with churches and marriage counseling centers to bring fun interactive activities to couples. For more information check us out at www.lauragethers.com/loveharder. You can also find her on Instagram and Facebook under the handle Love Harder Marriage Coaching.

Laura has a passion to truly see what God put together never separate. She believes that marriages can have a 100% success rate if men and women would use the Word of God to guard their hearts and protect their marriages. She believes that marriage is the toughest fight of your life. You constantly have to knock out anything that comes to destroy it. *May the Word of God and prayer be the weapons of choice as you fight for your marriage.*

@lovehardermarriagecoaching

30 Day Marriage Challenge

Day 1 - Kiss your spouse every time you see them.

Day 2 - Do whatever your spouse asks you to do as long as it doesn't cause you to sin against God.

Day 3 - Plan a romantic meal together.

Day 4 - Call or text your spouse throughout the day just to say I love you.

Day 5 - Only say edifying words to your spouse, give compliments, words or encouragement, etc.

Day 6 - Show a kind gesture towards your spouse.

Day 7 - Watch a TV show, or movie with your spouse.

Day 8 - Write your spouse a love letter.

Day 9 - Pray for your spouse throughout the day.

Day 10 - Sow into your spouse's dreams. (if they bake buy them some baking tools, if they like to exercise get them an article of clothing or pick up the kids so that they can get that extra time to work-out, whatever your spouse enjoys make sure you invest in it).

Day 11 - Read a scripture about marriage together and talk about it.

Day 12 - Read a love poem to each other.

Day 13 - Slow dance to your wedding/favorite song.

Day 14 - Do the laundry or dishes together.

Day 15 - Make something together.

Day 16 - Exercise together.

Day 17- Give each other a massage.

Day 18 - Watch a comedy show, or do something that will make you laugh together.

Day 19 - Turn off all electronic equipment and just talk to each other while in the home together.

Day 20- Take a shower/bath together.

Day 21- Play cards or a board game.

Day 22 - Buy a card for your spouse.

Day 23 - Prepare dinner together.

Day 24 - Hug each other every time you see one another.

Day 25- Look at your wedding photo album or video.

Day 26 - Write your spouse a poem.

Day 27- Do something spontaneous (if you have kids hire a baby sitter go and have some fun).

Day 28 - Sit and write a family vision statement or plan.

Day 29 - Complete a household chore your spouse is responsible for.

Day 30 - Turn out the lights and get busy (you can do this as often as you like you are married).